CHARLOTTE MEW

Selected Poems

821.8

BLOOMSBURY
* POETRY *
CLASSICS

This selection by Ian Hamilton
First published 1999

Copyright © 1999 by Bloomsbury Publishing Plc

Bloomsbury Publishing Plc, 38 Soho Square,
London W1V 5DF

A CIP catalogue record for this book
is available from the British Library

ISBN 0 7475 4607 X

10 9 8 7 6 5 4 3 2 1

Typeset in Great Britain by
Hewer Text Limited, Edinburgh
Printed in Great Britain by St Edmundsbury Press, Suffolk
Jacket design by Jeff Fisher

CONTENTS

INTRODUCTION

In a Preface to Charlotte Mew's *Collected Poems* (published by Duckworth in 1953), Alida Monro memorably describes her first meeting with the poet who would later become one of her closest friends. The date was November, 1915; the place: Harold Monro's then-celebrated Poetry Bookshop. Alida, Harold's wife, had been greatly impressed by the poem 'The Farmer's Bride' when it had appeared in *The Nation* magazine a couple of years earlier and she now wanted to persuade Mew to think about collecting her work together for a book. The Poetry Bookshop had its own imprint and was on the lookout for overlooked new talent: the gifted but neglected Mew seemed like a perfect candidate. A letter was sent, suggesting that the poet might attend one of the bookshop's Tuesday-evening readings. A non-committal answer came back and Alida had no expectation that the said-to-be-reclusive Mew would put in an appearance. But she did, and strikingly:

At about five minutes to six the swing door of the shop was pushed open and into the room stalked Charlotte Mew. Such a word best describes her walk. She was very small, only about four feet ten inches, very slight, with square shoulders and tiny hands and feet. She always wore a long double-breasted top-coat of tweed with a velvet collar inset. She usually carried a horn-handled umbrella, unrolled, under her arm, as if it were psychologically necessary to her, a weapon against the world. She had very fine white hair that showed traces of once having been a warm brown. Her eyes were a very dark grey, bright with black lashes and highly arched dark eyebrows. Her face was a fine oval, and she always wore a little hard felt pork-pie hat put on very straight. The whole time she was speaking she kept her eye cocked at a defiant angle. When she came into the shop she was asked: 'Are you Charlotte Mew?' and her reply, delivered characteristically with a slight smile of amusement, was; 'I am sorry to say I am.'

With some people, this response could have been taken as a foot-shuffling semi-affectation. With Charlotte Mew, the apology seemed heartfelt. This woman really didn't enjoy being who she was.

This much Alida could maybe have deduced from the few poems of Charlotte's she had read. In some of these, the sense of self-distaste, of an excludedness painful to endure but thoroughly deserved, was all too blatant. Now and then Mew could be shrill. In other poems, though, the author's sense of not belonging, of having to bear some deep spiritual disfigurement, seems chillingly stabilised, taken for granted. At this early stage of their relationship, Alida Monro knew next to nothing about Mew's background or her life, beyond what little she had gleaned from hearsay. The poet was in her mid-forties but for some years she had published very little. In 1915, what reputation she had was largely based on the none too original short stories she had contributed to Henry Harland's *Yellow Book* back in the 1890s, stories which had also never been collected. The poems, from the start, had been few and far between.

And yet, quite clearly, it was the poetry that mattered. It was like no one else's. There were echoes of Emily Brontë and Christina Rossetti, there was a touch of Hardy here and there, and there were signs too that Mew had taken notice of *Des Imagistes* (had not Ezra Pound accepted one of her poems for *The Egoist*?). But the intensity and pitch of Mew's address, her wobbly metres, her zigzag lineation, her use of impersonation to subdue a self she dared not give full rein to: all these were distinctively her own. Distinctive also was the sense that nearly all her poems bear of someone labouring beneath the weight of irreparable damage. Mew can be vividly, even gushingly, alive to nature, and to the passing human show, but intimations of death and madness are never very far away. They press in on her, as if to say: enjoy yourself if you have to, if you can, but don't pretend you're normal.

Mew's are the kind of poems that force readers to want to know about the author's life and personality. Alida Monro, certainly, wanted to know more. Or did she? Some of the hearsay she had gleaned was pretty challenging. It was said, for instance, that Mew had unhealthily strong connections with the various women's movements of the day, that she was unmarried, dressed like a man but had no men-friends, and so on. She had been a close ally of the feminist novelist May Sinclair, and on this matter there had been rumours of impropriety. Mew, so the story went, had made an impassioned pass at Sinclair and had been indignantly rebuffed. Sinclair had then made it her business to broadcast the ugly news. Was this – at least in part – the source of her low self-esteem? In spite of all the rumours,

Mew was known to be almost prissily moralistic, especially on sexual conduct. She would have been shocked, probably, if Sinclair had made a pass at her. If she had indeed, in this instance, succumbed to some errant impulse in her nature, she would have found it hard to bear the ensuing social shame. As Alida Monro puts it in her memoir: 'She had a strict moral code in respect of other people's conduct . . . and absolutely cut out from her friendship anyone on whom a breath of scandal blew.' Hence, perhaps, Mew's reluctance to expose herself to much public recognition.

In the event, Harold Monro's Poetry Bookshop did become Mew's first book publisher. Her first volume, *The Farmer's Bride*, appeared in 1916, and in the course of the book's preparation (which Mew monitored with some ferocity), Alida was vouchsafed at least an outline of her new author's unfortunate biography. Charlotte Mary Mew was born in London (at 30, Doughty Street) in 1869 and was the daughter of a moderately successful, rather spendthrift architect, one Frederick Mew. Her mother – Anna Maria Kendall – was the daughter of Frederick's partner, the somewhat more distinguished H. E. Kendall (Kendall was for some years surveyor of St Martin-in-the-Field). There were seven children of the Mew marriage, and Charlotte was the third. Of the other six, two boys died in infancy and another died in childhood, at the age of five. This five-year-old brother was only two years younger than little Charlotte and she was deeply affected by his sudden death. (See 'To a Child in Death'.)

She was devastated also by the fate of another brother,

Henry. Four years older than Charlotte and in childhood something of a hero-figure to his younger sister, Henry in his early twenties began to show signs of schizophrenia. The symptoms rapidly worsened and he was eventually confined to a mental hospital in Peckham, where he stayed until his death in 1901, aged thirty-six. Henry's tragedy looms fairly explicitly in poems like 'Ken', 'On the Asylum Road' and 'In Nunhead Cemetery' but it is also in the background of some of Mew's most anguished verse, even in those poems where she grapples with questions of religious belief and unbelief. In many of Mew's most intense poems, what seems to be a cry of loneliness is actually a plea for sanity, just as some of her most ardent prayers are prayers for the equilibrium of godlessness: 'I do not envy Him his victories. His arms are full of broken things.'

Also omnipresent in Mew's poems is the terrible question that Henry's fate gave rise to: is insanity inherited? The question had occurred to Mew quite early in her life because there was an uncle on her mother's side who showed signs of mental illness. It reared up again, of course, and forcefully, with Henry's illness – and then, not long before poor Henry's early death, was cruelly underscored when Charlotte's younger sister Freda (b. 1879) also had to be sent off to an asylum. Freda had been the beauty of the family, and her parents' favourite. Great things had been expected of her. Freda, though, never returned from the asylum. She lived to a great age and was in hospital for sixty years, uninterruptedly. The detail of Charlotte's poems 'Ken' and 'On the Asylum Road' are probably based on the visits she made to Freda's Isle of Wight asylum. In Mew's asylum poems, though, there is no suggestion that the lunatics she encounters should not have been locked away. Indeed, in one poem, she calls mad people 'the incarnate wages of man's sin'. For her, having a passionate, unruly nature was in some sense an affliction.

By the early 1900s, only two of the original seven Mew children were still living more or less sanely 'in the outside world': Charlotte and her sister Anne. But were *they* sane? Mew told Alida Monro that she and Anne 'had both made up their minds early in life that they would not marry for fear of passing on the mental taint that was in their family'. For Charlotte, of course, marriage was never very likely. Anne, though, seems to have been heterosexual and was still in her twenties when she elected to spend her life as Charlotte's full-time helpmate and companion. There is evidence that Charlotte sometimes felt guilty about Anne's sacrifice. One way of dealing with this guilt was to make much of Anne's talents as an artist. Anne did indeed paint, and enjoyed one or two modest successes, but she earned her living as a picture restorer and according to one Mew biographer 'was considered the most mentally stable of the family'.

In 1890, the Mew family – what was left of it – had moved from Doughty Street to Gordon Street, off Gordon Square in Bloomsbury. At first, the Mews were comfortably off but after Frederick Mew's death in 1898, the family was constantly beset by money worries. The Gordon Street house was big enough for them to take in lodgers – and this, reluctantly, was what they did. Housed in the upper floors, the lodgers were kept secret from the Mews' middle-class associates (as was the fate of Henry and Freda, whose hospitals the lodgers helped to pay for). The widowed Mrs Mew, together with Charlotte and Anne, and their pet parrot, lived on in Gordon Street until their lease expired, in 1922. They then moved to a smaller house in Camden (in Delancey Street) but after Mrs Mew's death in 1923, the sisters could not afford the rent of their new house and therefore decided to set up home in Anne's studio, off Charlotte Street.

This arrangement lasted for four years, and then the worst of all possible calamities occurred. Anne developed what seems to have been cancer of the liver and in January 1927 was told she had three months to live. In fact, she survived until June, with Charlotte frantically nursing her throughout her final months. When Anne died, aged fifty-six, Charlotte was not to be consoled. A year later she began to fall victim to the insanity she had dreaded all her life. 'She was unable to sleep', wrote Alida Monro, 'and so tortured herself with the idea that, as she had not had a vein opened in Anne's wrist, her sister might have been buried alive, that medical help had to be sought.' The doctors wanted Charlotte to be put into an asylum but she refused. In the end, she was admitted to a nursing home in Beaumont Street 'for a rest and medical supervision'. In February, 1928, Mew was installed in a dark, viewless room and told to rest. On March 24, writes Alida, 'she went out and bought a bottle of disinfectant and went back and swallowed it. In a brief moment of consciousness when doctors were trying to revive her, she said: "Don't keep me, let me go." It is melancholy to think that when her death was reported in the local Marylebone newspaper, she was casually described as "Charlotte New, said to be a writer".'

Two editions of *The Farmer's Bride* appeared during Charlotte Mew's lifetime. The second edition, published in 1921, included a dozen 'additional poems' (including two of her best: 'Saturday Market' and 'The Shade-Catchers'). A year after her death, another collection – *The Rambling Sailor* – was published by the Poetry Bookshop and carried a prefatory note signed 'A.K.' (presumably Alida Monro under her maiden name, which was Klementaski) and in 1953, twenty-five years after her death, came the *Collected Poems*.

During the last years of her life, Charlotte was often in touch with Thomas Hardy (and became good friends with his second wife) and Hardy's praise of her as 'the best living woman poet' has done much to keep her name alive. She remains, though, a neglected talent, remembered more for brilliant individual lines than for whole poems. Some of her longer pieces can seem too frantic and directionless and maybe this is the price we have to pay for her unnerving candour. At her best, though, and when she is fully in control of her material, she seems to me to be one of our most affecting and authentic modern poets. Certainly, both as poet and as literary phenomenon, she has to be classed as an original of lasting value.

Ian Hamilton

AT THE CONVENT GATE

'Why do you shrink away, and start and stare?
    Life frowns to see you leaning at death's gate –
  Not back, but on. Ah! sweet, it is too late:
You cannot cast these kisses from your hair.
Will God's cold breath blow kindly anywhere
  Upon such burning gold? Oh! lips worn white
  With waiting! Love will blossom in a night
And you shall wake to find the roses there!'

'Oh hush! He seems to stir, He lifts His Head.
He smiles. Look where He hangs against the sky.
He never smiled nor stirred, that God of pain
With tired eyes and limbs above my bed –
But loose me, this is death, I will not die –
Not while He smiles. Oh! Christ, Thine own again!'

REQUIESCAT

Your birds that call from tree to tree
   Just overhead, and whirl and dart,
Your breeze fresh-blowing from the sea,
   And your sea singing on, Sweetheart.

Your salt scent on the thin sharp air
   Of this grey dawn's first drowsy hours,
While on the grass shines everywhere
   The yellow starlight of your flowers.

At the road's end your strip of blue
   Beyond that line of naked trees –
Strange that we should remember you
   As if you would remember these!

As if your spirit, swaying yet
   To the old passions, were not free
Of Spring's wild magic, and the fret
   Of the wilder wooing of the sea!

What threat of old imaginings,
   Half-haunted joy, enchanted pain,
Or dread of unfamiliar things
   Should ever trouble you again?

Yet you would wake and want, you said,
    The little whirl of wings, the clear
Gay notes, the wind, the golden bed
    Of the daffodil: and they are here!

Just overhead, they whirl and dart
    Your birds that call from tree to tree,
Your sea is singing on – Sweetheart,
    Your breeze is blowing from the sea.

Beyond the line of naked trees
    At the road's end, your stretch of blue –
Strange if you should remember these
    As we, ah! God! remember you!

THE LITTLE PORTRESS
(St. Gilda de Rhuys)

The stillness of the sunshine lies
   Upon her spirit: silence seems
   To look out from its place of dreams
When suddenly she lifts her eyes
   To waken, for a little space,
   The smile asleep upon her face.

A thousand years of sun and shower,
   The melting of unnumbered snows
   Go to the making of the rose
Which blushes out its little hour.
   So old is Beauty: in its heart
   The ages seem to meet and part.

Like Beauty's self, she holds a clear
   Deep memory of hidden things –
   The music of forgotten springs –
So far she travels back, so near
   She seems to stand to patient truth
   As old as Age, as young as Youth.

That is her window, by the gate.
  Now and again her figure flits
  Across the wall. Long hours she sits
Within: on all who come to wait.
  Her Saviour too is hanging there
  A foot or so above her chair.

'Sœur Marie de l'enfant Jésus,'
  You wrote it in my little book –
  Your shadow-name. Your shadow-look
Is dimmer and diviner too,
  But not to keep: it slips so far
  Beyond us to that golden bar

Where angels, watching from their stair,
  Half-envy you your tranquil days
  Of prayer as exquisite as praise, –
Grey twilights softer than their glare
  Of glory: all sweet human things
  Which vanish with the whirr of wings.

Yet will you, when you wing your way
  To whiter worlds, more whitely shine
  Or shed a radiance more divine
Than here you shed from day to day –
  High in His heaven a quiet star,
  Be nearer God than now you are?

AFTERNOON TEA

Please you, excuse me, good five-o'clock people,
   I've lost my last hatful of words,
And my heart's in the wood up above the church
   steeple,
   I'd rather have tea with the birds.

Gay Kate's stolen kisses, poor Barnaby's scars,
   John's losses and Mary's gains,
Oh! what do they matter, my dears, to the stars
   Or the glow-worms in the lanes!

I'd rather lie under the tall elm-trees,
   With old rooks talking loud overhead,
To watch a red squirrel run over my knees,
   Very still on my brackeny bed.

And wonder what feathers the wrens will be taking
   For lining their nests next Spring;
Or why the tossed shadow of boughs in a great wind
   shaking
   Is such a lovely thing.

SHE WAS A SINNER

Love was my flower, and before He came –
   'Master, there was a garden where it grew
Rank, with the colour of a crimson flame,
   Thy flower too, but knowing not its name
Nor yet that it was Thine, I did not spare
But tore and trampled it and stained my hair,
My hands, my lips, with the red petals; see,
   Drenched with the blood of Thy poor murdered
   flower
I stood, when suddenly the hour
           Struck for me,
And straight I came and wound about Thy Feet
           The strands of shame
Twined with those broken buds: till lo, more sweet,
           More red, yet still the same,
Bright burning blossoms sprang around Thy brow
Beneath the thorns (I saw, I know not how,
The crown which Thou wast afterward to wear
           On that immortal Tree)
And I went out and found my garden very bare,
But swept and watered it, then followed Thee.

There was another garden where to seek
Thee, first, I came in those grey hours
Of the Great Dawn, and knew Thee not till Thou
    didst speak
My name, that "Mary" like a flash of light
Shot from Thy lips. Thou wast "the gardener" too,
                And then I knew
That evermore our flowers,
Thine, Lord, and mine, shall be a burning white.'

TO A LITTLE CHILD IN DEATH

Dear, if little feet make little journeys,
  Thine should not be far;
    Though beyond the faintest star,
    Past earth's last bar,
    Where angels are,
      Thou hast to travel –
Cross the far blue spaces of the sea,
Climb above the tallest tree,
Higher up than many mountains be;
  Sure there is some shorter way for thee,
Since little feet make little journeys.

Then, if smallest limbs are soonest weary,
  Thou should'st soon be there;
    Stumbling up the golden stair,
    Where the angels' shining hair

    Brushes dust from baby faces.
Very, very gently cling
To a silver-edged wing,
  And peep from under.
Then thou'lt see the King,
Then will many voices sing,
  And thou wilt wonder.

Wait a little while
For Him to smile,
Who calleth thee.
He who calleth all,
Both great and small,
From over mountain, star and sea,
Doth call the smallest soonest to His knee,
Since smallest limbs are soonest weary.

PÉRI EN MER
(Camaret)

One day the friends who stand about my bed
    Will slowly turn from it to speak of me
Indulgently, as of the newly dead,
    Not knowing how I perished by the sea,
That night in summer when the gulls topped white
    The crowded masts cut black against a sky
Of fading rose – where suddenly the light
    Of Youth went out, and I, no longer I,
Climbed home, the homeless ghost I was to be.
    Yet as I passed, they sped me up the heights –
Old seamen round the door of the Abrí
    De la Tempête. Even on quiet nights
    So may some ship go down with all her lights
Beyond the sight of watchers on the quay!

THE FARMER'S BRIDE

Three Summers since I chose a maid,
Too young maybe – but more's to do
At harvest-time than bide and woo.
    When us was wed she turned afraid
Of love and me and all things human;
Like the shut of a winter's day.
Her smile went out, and 'twasn't a woman –
    More like a little frightened fay.
        One night, in the Fall, she runned away.

'Out 'mong the sheep, her be,' they said,
'Should properly have been abed;
But sure enough she wasn't there
Lying awake with her wide brown stare.
So over seven-acre field and up-along across the down
    We chased her, flying like a hare
Before our lanterns. To Church-Town
    All in a shiver and a scare
We caught her, fetched her home at last
    And turned the key upon her, fast.

She does the work about the house
As well as most, but like a mouse:
    Happy enough to chat and play
    With birds and rabbits and such as they,
    So long as men-folk keep away.
'Not near, not near!' her eyes beseech

When one of us comes within reach.
  The women say that beasts in stall
  Look round like children at her call.
  I've hardly heard her speak at all.

Shy as a leveret, swift as he,
Straight and slight as a young larch tree,
Sweet as the first wild violets, she,
To her wild self. But what to me?

The short days shorten and the oaks are brown,
  The blue smoke rises to the low grey sky,
One leaf in the still air falls slowly down,
  A magpie's spotted feathers lie
On the black earth spread white with rime,
The berries redden up to Christmas-time.
  What's Christmas-time without there be
  Some other in the house than we!

  She sleeps up in the attic there
  Alone, poor maid. 'Tis but a stair
Betwixt us. Oh! my God! the down
  The soft young down of her, the brown,
The brown of her – her eyes, her hair, her hair!

FAME

Sometimes in the over-heated house, but not for long,
    Smirking and speaking rather loud,
  I see myself among the crowd,
Where no one fits the singer to his song,
Or sifts the unpainted from the painted faces
Of the people who are always on my stair;
They were not with me when I walked in heavenly places;
    But could I spare
In the blind Earth's great silences and spaces,
    The din, the scuffle, the long stare
    If I went back and it was not there?
Back to the old known things that are the new,
The folded glory of the gorse, the sweet-briar air,
To the larks that cannot praise us, knowing nothing of
    what we do
    And the divine, wise trees that do not care
Yet, to leave Fame, still with such eyes and that bright
    hair!
God! If I might! And before I go hence
    Take in her stead
    To our tossed bed,
One little dream, no matter how small, how wild.
Just now, I think I found it in a field, under a fence –
A frail, dead, new-born lamb, ghostly and pitiful and
    white,
    A blot upon the night,
    The moon's dropped child!

THE NARROW DOOR

The narrow door, the narrow door
On the three steps of which the café children play
Mostly at shop with pebbles from the shore,
It is always shut this narrow door
But open for a little while to-day.

And round it, each with pebbles in his hand,
A silenced crowd the café children stand
To see the long box jerking down the bend
Of twisted stair; then set on end,
Quite filling up the narrow door
Till it comes out and does not go in any more.

Along the quay you see it wind,
The slow black line. Someone pulls up the blind
Of the small window just above the narrow door –
    'Tiens! que veux-tu acheter?' Renée cries,
    'Mais, pour quat'sous, des oignons,' Jean replies
And one pays down with pebbles from the shore.

THE FÊTE

To-night again the moon's white mat
    Stretches across the dormitory floor
While outside, like an evil cat
    The *pion* prowls down the dark corridor,
    Planning, I know, to pounce on me, in spite
For getting leave to sleep in town last night.
But it was none of us who made that noise,
    Only the old brown owl that hoots and flies
Out of the ivy – he will say it was us boys –
    Seigneur mon Dieu! the *sacré* soul of spies!
    He would like to catch each dream that lies
        Hidden behind our sleepy eyes:
Their dream? But mine – it is the moon and the wood
    that sees;
All my long life how I shall hate the trees!

In the *Place d'Armes*, the dusty planes, all Summer
    through
Dozed with the market women in the sun and scarcely
    stirred
    To see the quiet things that crossed the Square –,
A tiny funeral, the flying shadow of a bird,
    The hump-backed barber Célestin Lemaire,
    Old madame Michel in her three-wheeled chair,
        And filing past to Vespers, two and two,
        The *demoiselles* of the *pensionnat*.

Towed like a ship through the harbour bar,
    Safe into port, where *le petit Jésus*
Perhaps makes nothing of the look they shot at you:
    Si, c'est défendu, mais que voulez-vous?
It was the sun. The sunshine weaves
A pattern on dull stones: the sunshine leaves
    The portraiture of dreams upon the eyes
        Before it dies:
    All Summer through
The dust hung white upon the drowsy planes
Till suddenly they woke with the Autumn rains.

It is not only the little boys
    Who have hardly got away from toys,
But I, who am seventeen next year,
Some nights, in bed, have grown cold to hear
    That lonely passion of the rain
Which makes you think of being dead,
And of somewhere living to lay your head
    As if you were a child again,
Crying for one thing, known and near
Your empty heart, to still the hunger and the fear
    That pelts and beats with it against the pane.

But I remember smiling too
At all the sun's soft tricks and those Autumn dreads
    In winter time, when the grey light broke slowly
    through
The frosted window-lace to drag us shivering from our beds.

And when at dusk the singing wind swung down
Straight from the stars to the dark country roads
    Beyond the twinkling town,
  Striking the leafless poplar boughs as he went by,
Like some poor, stray dog by the wayside lying dead,
We left behind us the old world of dread,
I and the wind as we strode whistling on under the
    Winter sky.

And then in Spring for three days came the Fair
  Just as the planes were starting into bud
Above the caravans: you saw the dancing bear
    Pass on his chain; and heard the jingle and the
    thud.
    Only four days ago
    They let you out of this dull show
To slither down the *montagne russe* and chaff the man
  à la tête de veau –
    Hit, slick, the bull's eye at the *tir*,
Spin round and round till your head went queer
On the *porcs-roulants*. Oh! *là là! la fête*
Va pour du vin, et le tête-à-tête
With the girl who sugars the *gaufres! Pauvrette*,
  How thin she was; but she smiled, you bet,
  As she took your tip – 'One does not forget
The good days, Monsieur.' Said with a grace,
But *sacrebleu!* what a ghost of a face!
  And no fun too for the *demoiselles*

34

Of the *pensionnat*, who were hurried past,
    With their 'Oh, *que c'est beau – Ah, qu'elle est belle!*'
A lap-dog's life from first to last!
The good nights are not made for sleep, nor the good
    days for dreaming in,
        And at the end in the big Circus tent we sat and
        shook and stewed like sin!

    Some children there had got – but where?
Sent from the south, perhaps – a red bouquet
    Of roses, sweetening the fetid air
With scent from gardens by some far away blue bay.
    They threw one at the dancing bear;
The white clown caught it. From St. Rémy's tower
    The deep, slow bell tolled out the hour;
The black clown, with his dirty grin
    Lay, sprawling in the dust, as She rode in.

She stood on a white horse – and suddenly you saw
    the bend
Of a far-off road at dawn, with knights riding by,
A field of spears – and then the gallant day
Go out in storm, with ragged clouds low down, sullen
    and grey
        Against red heavens: wild and awful, such a sky
        As witnesses against you at the end
Of a great battle; bugles blowing, blood and dust –
The *old Morte d'Arthur*, fight you must –.

It died in anger. But it was not death
That had you by the throat, stopping your breath.
She looked like Victory. She rode my way.

She laughed at the black clown and then she flew
    A bird above us, on the wing
Of her white arms; and you saw through
A rent in the old tent, a patch of sky
With one dim star. She flew, but not so high –
    And then she did not fly;
She stood in the bright moonlight at the door
Of a strange room, she threw her slippers on the
   floor –
      Again, again
   You heard the patter of the rain,
   The starving rain – it was this Thing,
Summer was this, the gold mist in your eyes; –
    Oh God! it dies,
    But after death –,
  To-night the splendour and the sting
  Blows back and catches at your breath,
The smell of beasts, the smell of dust, the scent of all
  the roses in the world, the sea, the Spring,
The beat of drums, the pad of hoofs, music, the
  dream, the dream, the Enchanted Thing!

At first you scarcely saw her face,
    You knew the maddening feet were there,
What called was that half-hidden, white unrest
To which now and then she pressed
    Her finger tips; but as she slackened pace
    And turned and looked at you it grew quite bare:
        There was not anything you did not dare: –
Like trumpeters the hours passed until the last day of
    the Fair.

In the *Place d'Armes* all afternoon
    The building birds had sung 'Soon, soon,'
The shuttered streets slept sound that night,
        It was full moon:
The path into the wood was almost white,
The trees were very still and seemed to stare:
    Not far before your soul the Dream flits on,
    But when you touch it, it is gone
And quite alone your soul stands there.

Mother of Christ, no one has seen your eyes: how can
    men pray
        Even unto you?
There were only wolves' eyes in the wood –
        My Mother is a woman too:
Nothing is true that is not good,
With that quick smile of hers, I have heard her say; –
I wish I had gone back home to-day;
    I should have watched the light that so gently dies

37

From our high window, in the Paris skies,
     The long, straight chain
Of lamps hung out along the Seine:
I would have turned to her and let the rain
Beat on her breast as it does against the pane; –
     Nothing will be the same again; –
There is something strange in my little Mother's eyes,
There is something new in the old heavenly air of
     Spring –
The smell of beasts, the smell of dust – *The Enchanted
     Thing!*

All my life long I shall see moonlight on the fern
     And the black trunks of trees. Only the hair
Of any woman can belong to God.
The stalks are cruelly broken where we trod,
     There had been violets there,
     I shall not care
As I used to do when I see the bracken burn.

BESIDE THE BED

Someone has shut the shining eyes, straightened and
    folded
    The wandering hands quietly covering the unquiet
    breast:
So, smoothed and silenced you lie, like a child, not
    again to be questioned or scolded;
    But, for you, not one of us believes that this is rest.

Not so to close the windows down can cloud and
    deaden
    The blue beyond: or to screen the wavering flame
    subdue its breath:
Why, if I lay my cheek to your cheek, your grey lips,
    like dawn, would quiver and redden,
    Breaking into the old, odd smile at this fraud of
    death.

Because all night you have not turned to us or spoken
    It is time for you to wake; your dreams were never
    very deep:
I, for one, have seen the thin, bright, twisted threads
    of them dimmed suddenly and broken,
    This is only a most piteous pretence of sleep!

IN NUNHEAD CEMETERY

It is the clay that makes the earth stick to his spade;
  He fills in holes like this year after year;
The others have gone; they were tired, and half afraid,
  But I would rather be standing here;

There is nowhere else to go. I have seen this place
  From the windows of the train that's going past
Against the sky. This is rain on my face –
  It was raining here when I saw it last.

There is something horrible about a flower;
  This, broken in my hand, is one of those
He threw in just now: it will not live another hour;
  There are thousands more: you do not miss a rose.

One of the children hanging about
  Pointed at the whole dreadful heap and smiled
This morning, after THAT was carried out;
  There is something terrible about a child.

We were like children, last week, in the Strand;
  That was the day you laughed at me
Because I tried to make you understand
  The cheap, stale chap I used to be
  Before I saw the things you made me see.

This is not a real place; perhaps by-and-by
    I shall wake – I am getting drenched with all this
    rain:
To-morrow I will tell you about the eyes of the Crystal
    Palace train
    Looking down on us, and you will laugh and I shall
    see what you see again.

Not here, not now. We said 'Not yet
Across our low stone parapet
Will the quick shadows of the sparrows fall.'

But still it was a lovely thing
Through the grey months to wait for Spring
With the birds that go a-gypsying
In the parks till the blue seas call.
And next to these, you used to care
For the lions in Trafalgar Square,
Who'll stand and speak for London when her bell of
    Judgment tolls –
        And the gulls at Westminster that were
        The old sea-captains' souls.
To-day again the brown tide splashes, step by step, the
    river stair,
        And the gulls are there!

By a month we have missed our Day:
    The children would have hung about
Round the carriage and over the way
    As you and I came out.

We should have stood on the gulls' black cliffs and
        heard the sea
    And seen the moon's white track,
I would have called, you would have come to me
    And kissed me back.

You have never done that: I do not know
    Why I stood staring at your bed
And heard you, though you spoke so low,
    But could not reach your hands, your little head.
There was nothing we could not do, you said,
    And you went, and I let you go!

Now I will burn you back, I will burn you through,
    Though I am damned for it we two will lie
    And burn, here where the starlings fly
    To these white stones from the wet sky - ;
    Dear, you will say this is not I -
It would not be you, it would not be you!

If for only a little while
    You will think of it you will understand,
    If you will touch my sleeve and smile
As you did that morning in the Strand
    I can wait quietly with you
    Or go away if you want me to –
God! What is God? but your face has gone and
your hand!
    Let me stay here too.

When I was quite a little lad
At Christmas time we went half mad
For joy of all the toys we had,
And then we used to sing about the sheep
    The shepherds watched by night;
We used to pray to Christ to keep
    Our small souls safe till morning light – ;
I am scared, I am staying with you to-night –
                    Put me to sleep.

I shall stay here: here you can see the sky;
The houses in the streets are much too high;
    There is no one left to speak to there;
    Here they are everywhere,
And just above them fields and fields of roses lie –
If he would dig it all up again they would not die.

PÉCHERESSE

Down the long quay the slow boats glide,
    While here and there a house looms white
Against the gloom of the waterside,
    And some high window throws a light
    As they sail out into the night.

At dawn they will bring in again
    To women knitting on the quay
Who wait for him, their man of men;
    I stand with them, and watch the sea
    Which may have taken mine from me.

Just so the long days come and go.
    The nights, ma Doué! the nights are cold!
Our Lady's heart is as frozen snow,
    Since this one sin I have not told;
    And I shall die or perhaps grow old

Before he comes. The foreign ships
    Bring many a one of face and name
As strange as his, to buy your lips,
    A gold piece for a scarlet shame
    Like mine. But mine was not the same.

One night was ours, one short grey day
　　Of sudden sin, unshrived, untold.
He found me, and I lost the way
　　To Paradise for him. I sold
　　My soul for love and not for gold.

He bought my soul, but even so,
　　My face is all that he has seen,
His is the only face I know,
And in the dark church, like a screen,
　　It shuts God out; it comes between;

While in some narrow foreign street
　　Or loitering on the crowded quay,
Who knows what others he may meet
　　To turn his eyes away from me?
　　Many are fair to such as he!

There is but one for such as I
　　To love, to hate, to hunger for;
I shall, perhaps, grow old and die,
　　With one short day to spend and store,
　　One night, in all my life, no more.

Just so the long days come and go,
　　Yet this one sin I will not tell
Though Mary's heart is as frozen snow
And all nights are cold for one warmed too well.
　　But, oh! ma Doué! *the nights of Hell!*

THE CHANGELING

Toll no bell for me, dear Father, dear Mother,
    Waste no sighs;
There are my sisters, there is my little brother
    Who plays in the place called Paradise,
Your children all, your children for ever;
        But I, so wild,
Your disgrace, with the queer brown face, was never,
    Never, I know, but half your child!

In the garden at play, all day, last summer,
        Far and away I heard
The sweet 'tweet-tweet' of a strange new-comer,
    The dearest, clearest call of a bird.
It lived down there in the deep green hollow,
    My own old home, and the fairies say
The word of a bird is a thing to follow,
    So I was away a night and a day.

One evening, too, by the nursery fire,
    We snuggled close and sat round so still,
When suddenly as the wind blew higher,
    Something scratched on the window-sill.
A pinched brown face peered in – I shivered;
    No one listened or seemed to see;
The arms of it waved and the wings of it quivered,
    Whoo – I knew it had come for me;
    Some are as bad as bad can be!

All night long they danced in the rain,
Round and round in a dripping chain,
Threw their caps at the window-pane,
Tried to make me scream and shout
And fling the bedclothes all about:
I meant to stay in bed that night,
And if only you had left a light
They would never have got me out.

Sometimes I wouldn't speak, you see,
Or answer when you spoke to me,
Because in the long, still dusks of Spring
You can hear the whole world whispering;
The shy green grasses making love,
The feathers grow on the dear, grey dove,
The tiny heart of the redstart beat,
The patter of the squirrel's feet,
The pebbles pushing in the silver streams,
The rushes talking in their dreams,
The swish-swish of the bat's black wings,
The wild-wood bluebell's sweet ting-tings,
Humming and hammering at your ear,
Everything there is to hear
In the heart of hidden things,
But not in the midst of the nursery riot,
That's why I wanted to be quiet,
Couldn't do my sums, or sing,
Or settle down to anything.

And when, for that, I was sent upstairs
   I *did* kneel down to say my prayers;
But the King who sits on your high church steeple
Has nothing to do with us fairy people!

'Times I pleased you, dear Father, dear Mother,
   Learned all my lessons and liked to play,
And dearly loved the little pale brother
   Whom some other bird must have called away.
Why did They bring me here to make me
   Not quite bad and not quite good,
Why, unless They're wicked, do They want, in spite,
   to take me
   Back to their wet, wild wood?
Now, every night I shall see the windows shining,
   The gold lamp's glow, and the fire's red gleam,
While the best of us are twining twigs and the rest of
   us are whining
     In the hollow by the stream.
Black and chill are Their nights on the wold;
   And They live so long and They feel no pain:
I shall grow up, but never grow old,
I shall always, always be very cold,
     I shall never come back again!

KEN

The town is old and very steep,
    A place of bells and cloisters and grey towers,
And black clad people walking in their sleep –
    A nun, a priest, a woman taking flowers
    To her new grave; and watched from end to end
    By the great Church above, through the still hours:
        But in the morning and the early dark

The children wake to dart from doors and call
Down the wide, crooked street, where, at the bend,
    Before it climbs up to the park,
Ken's is the gabled house facing the Castle wall.

When first I came upon him there
Suddenly, on the half-lit stair,
I think I hardly found a trace
Of likeness to a human face
    In his. And I said then
If in His image God made men,
Some other must have made poor Ken –
But for his eyes which looked at you
As two red, wounded stars might do.

He scarcely spoke, you scarcely heard,
  His voice broke off in little jars
To tears sometimes. An uncouth bird
  He seemed as he ploughed up the street,
Groping, with knarred, high-lifted feet
  And arms thrust out as if to beat
    Always against a threat of bars.

And oftener than not there'd be
A child just higher than his knee
Trotting beside him. Through his dim
  Long twilight this, at least, shone clear,
  That all the children and the deer,
    Whom every day he went to see
Out in the park, belonged to him.

  'God help the folk that next him sits
    He fidgets so, with his poor wits.'
The neighbours said on Sunday nights
When he would go to Church to 'see the lights!'
  Although for these he used to fix
  His eyes upon a crucifix
  In a dark corner, staring on
  Till everybody else had gone.
  And sometimes, in his evil fits,
You could not move him from his chair –
You did not look at him as he sat there,
  Biting his rosary to bits.
While pointing to the Christ he tried to say
    'Take it away.'

Nothing was dead:
He said 'a bird' if he picked up a broken wing,
    A perished leaf or any such thing
        Was just 'a rose'; and once when I had said
    He must not stand and knock there any more,
    He left a twig on the mat outside my door.

    Not long ago
The last thrush stiffened in the snow,
    While black against a sullen sky
        The sighing pines stood by.
But now the wind has left our rattled pane
To flutter the hedge-sparrow's wing,
The birches in the wood are red again
        And only yesterday
The larks went up a little way to sing
        What lovers say
    Who loiter in the lanes to-day;
    The buds begin to talk of May
    With learned rooks on city trees,
    And if God please
        With all of these
We too, shall see another Spring.

But in that red brick barn upon the hill
    I wonder – can one own the deer,
    And does one walk with children still
        As one did here –
        Do roses grow
Beneath those twenty windows in a row –

And if some night
When you have not seen any light
They cannot move you from your chair
    What happens there?
        I do not know.

        So, when they took
Ken to that place, I did not look
        After he called and turned on me
        His eyes. These I shall see –

À QUOI BON DIRE

Seventeen years ago you said
　　Something that sounded like Good-bye;
　　And everybody thinks that you are dead,
　　　　But I.

So I, as I grow stiff and cold
To this and that say Good-bye too;
　　And everybody sees that I am old
　　　　But you.

And one fine morning in a sunny lane
Some boy and girl will meet and kiss and swear
　　That nobody can love their way again
　　　　While over there
You will have smiled, I shall have tossed your hair.

THE QUIET HOUSE

When we were children old Nurse used to say,
   The house was like an auction or a fair
Until the lot of us were safe in bed.
   It has been quiet as the country-side
   Since Ted and Janey and then Mother died
And Tom crossed Father and was sent away.
After the lawsuit he could not hold up his head,
   Poor Father, and he does not care
   For people here, or to go anywhere.

To get away to Aunt's for that week-end
   Was hard enough; (since then, a year ago,
   He scarcely lets me slip out of his sight –)
At first I did not like my cousin's friend,
   I did not think I should remember him:
   His voice has gone, his face is growing dim
And if I like him now I do not know.
   He frightened me before he smiled –
   He did not ask me if he might –
   He said that he would come one Sunday night,
   He spoke to me as if I were a child.

No year has been like this that has just gone by;
   It may be that what Father says is true,
If things are so it does not matter why:
   But everything has burned, and not quite through.

The colours of the world have turned
To flame, the blue, the gold has burned
In what used to be such a leaden sky.
When you are burned quite through you die.

Red is the strangest pain to bear;
In Spring the leaves on the budding trees;
In Summer the roses are worse than these,
    More terrible than they are sweet:
    A rose can stab you across the street
        Deeper than any knife:
    And the crimson haunts you everywhere –
Thin shafts of sunlight, like the ghosts of reddened
    swords have struck our stair
As if, coming down, you had split your life.

I think that my soul is red
Like the soul of a sword or a scarlet flower:
    But when these are dead
    They have had their hour.

I shall have had mine, too,
    For from head to feet,
I am burned and stabbed half through,
    And the pain is deadly sweet.

The things that kill us seem
    Blind to the death they give:
It is only in our dream
    The things that kill us live.

The room is shut where Mother died,
  The other rooms are as they were,
The world goes on the same outside,
  The sparrows fly across the Square,
  The children play as we four did there,
  The trees grow green and brown and bare,
The sun shines on the dead Church spire,
  And nothing lives here but the fire,
While Father watches from his chair
      Day follows day
The same, or now and then, a different grey,
      Till, like his hair,
Which Mother said was wavy once and bright,
      They will all turn white.

  To-night I heard a bell again –
Outside it was the same mist of fine rain,
The lamps just lighted down the long, dim street,
      No one for me –
  I think it is myself I go to meet:
I do not care; some day I *shall* not think; I shall not *be*!

ON THE ASYLUM ROAD

Theirs is the house whose windows – every pane –
    Are made of darkly stained or clouded glass:
Sometimes you come upon them in the lane,
    The saddest crowd that you will ever pass.

But still we merry town or village folk
    Throw to their scattered stare a kindly grin,
And think no shame to stop and crack a joke
    With the incarnate wages of man's sin.

None but ourselves in our long gallery we meet,
    The moor-hen stepping from her reeds with dainty feet,
        The hare-bell bowing on his stem,
Dance not with us; their pulses beat
    To fainter music; nor do we to them
        Make their life sweet.

The gayest crowd that they will ever pass
    Are we to brother-shadows in the lane:
Our windows, too, are clouded glass
    To them, yes, every pane!

JOUR DES MORTS
(Cimetière Montparnasse)

Sweetheart, is this the last of all our posies
   And little festivals, my flowers are they
But white and wistful ghosts of gayer roses
   Shut with you in this grim garden? Not to-day,
Ah! no! come out with me before the grey gate closes
   It is your fête and here is your bouquet!

THE FOREST ROAD

The forest road,
The infinite straight road stretching away
World without end: the breathless road between the
    walls
Of the black listening trees: the hushed, grey road
Beyond the window that you shut to-night
Crying that you would look at it by day –
There is a shadow there that sings and calls
But not for you. Oh! hidden eyes that plead in sleep
Against the lonely dark, if I could touch the fear
And leave it kissed away on quiet lids –
If I could hush these hands that are half-awake,
Groping for me in sleep I could go free.
I wish that God would take them out of mine
And fold them like the wings of frightened birds
Shot cruelly down, but fluttering into quietness so soon,
Broken, forgotten things; there is no grief for them in
    the green Spring
When the new birds fly back to the old trees.
But it shall not be so with you. I will look back. I wish
    I knew that God would stand
Smiling and looking down on you when morning
    comes,
To hold you, when you wake, closer than I,
So gently though: and not with famished lips or
    hungry arms:
He does not hurt the frailest, dearest things

As we do in the dark. See, dear, your hair –
I must unloose this hair that sleeps and dreams
About my face, and clings like the brown weed
To drowned, delivered things, tossed by the tired sea
Back to the beaches. Oh! your hair! If you had lain
A long time dead on the rough, glistening ledge
Of some black cliff, forgotten by the tide,
The raving winds would tear, the dripping brine would
    rust away
Fold after fold of all the loveliness
That wraps you round, and makes you, lying here,
The passionate fragrance that the roses are.
But death would spare the glory of your head
In the long sweetness of the hair that does not die:
The spray would leap to it in every storm,
The scent of the unsilenced sea would linger on
In these dark waves, and round the silence that was you –
Only the nesting gulls would hear – but there would
    still be whispers in your hair;
Keep them for me; keep them for me. What *is* this
    singing on the road
That makes all other music like the music in a dream –
Dumb to the dancing and the marching feet; you
    know, in dreams, you see
Old pipers playing that you cannot hear,
And ghostly drums that only seem to beat. This seems
    to climb:
Is it the music of a larger place? It makes our room too
    small: it is like a stair,

A calling stair that climbs up to a smile you scarcely
  see,
Dim, but so waited for; and *you* know what a smile is,
  how it calls,
How if I smiled you always ran to me.
Now you must sleep forgetfully, as children do.
There is a Spirit sits by us in sleep
Nearer than those who walk with us in the bright day.
I think he has a tranquil, saving face: I think he came
Straight from the hills: he may have suffered there in
  time gone by,
And once, from those forsaken heights, looked down,
Lonely himself, on all the lonely sorrows of the earth.
It is his kingdom – Sleep. If I could leave you there –
If, without waking you, I could get up and reach the
  door – !
We used to go together. – Shut, scared eyes,
Poor, desolate, desperate hands, it is not I
Who thrust you off. No, take your hands away –
I cannot strike your lonely hands. Yes, I have struck
  your heart,
It did not come so near. Then lie you there
Dear and wild heart behind this quivering snow
With two red stains on it: and I will strike and tear
Mine out, and scatter it to yours. Oh! throbbing dust,
You that were life, our little wind-blown hearts!
                    The road! the road!
There is a shadow there: I see my soul,
I hear my soul, singing among the trees!

61

MADELEINE IN CHURCH

Here, in the darkness, where this plaster saint
   Stands nearer than God stands to our distress,
And one small candle shines, but not so faint
   As the far lights of everlastingness
I'd rather kneel than over there, in open day
     Where Christ is hanging, rather pray
       To something more like my own clay,
         Not too divine;
       For, once, perhaps my little saint
       Before he got his niche and crown,
   Had one short stroll about the town;
   It brings him closer, just that taint
     And anyone can wash the paint
Off our poor faces, his and mine!

Is that why I see Monty now? equal to any saint, poor
   boy, as good as gold,
But still, with just the proper trace
Of earthliness on his shining wedding face;
And then gone suddenly blank and old
The hateful day of the divorce:
Stuart got his, hands down, of course
Crowing like twenty cocks and grinning like a horse:
But Monty took it hard. All said and done I liked him
   best, –
He was the first, he stands out clearer than the rest.

It seems too funny all we other rips
  Should have immortal souls; Monty and Redge
    quite damnably
  Keep theirs afloat while we go down like scuttled
    ships. –
      It's funny too, how easily we sink,
      One might put up a monument, I think
    To half the world and cut across it 'Lost at Sea!'
I should drown Jim, poor little sparrow, if I netted him
  to-night –
      No, it's no use this penny light –
      Or my poor saint with his tin-pot crown –
    The trees of Calvary are where they were,
      When we are sure that we can spare
      The tallest, let us go and strike it down
    And leave the other two still standing there.
      I, too, would ask Him to remember me
If there were any Paradise beyond this earth that I
  could see.

      Oh! quiet Christ who never knew
      The poisonous fangs that bite us through
        And make us do the things we do,
      See how we suffer and fight and die,
      How helpless and how low we lie,
      God holds You, and You hang so high,
      Though no one looking long at You,
        Can think You do not suffer too,

But, up there, from your still, star-lighted tree
   What can You know, what can You really see
      Of this dark ditch, the soul of me!

    We are what we are: when I was half a child I
      could not sit
Watching black shadows on green lawns and red
   carnations burning in the sun,
         Without paying so heavily for it
   That joy and pain, like any mother and her unborn
    child were almost one.
         I could hardly bear
     The dreams upon the eyes of white geraniums
      in the dusk,
       The thick, close voice of musk,
       The jessamine music on the thin night air,
     Or, sometimes, my own hands about me
      anywhere –
The sight of my own face (for it was lovely then) even
   the scent of my own hair,
   Oh! there was nothing, nothing that did not sweep
    to the high seat
    Of laughing gods, and then blow down and beat
My soul into the highway dust, as hoofs do the
   dropped roses of the street.

I think my body was my soul,
　　And when we are made thus
　　　　Who shall control
Our hands, our eyes, the wandering passion of
　　　our feet,
　　　　Who shall teach us
To thrust the world out of our heart; to say, till
　perhaps in death,
　　　　　When the race is run,
And it is forced from us with our last breath
　　　　'Thy will be done'?
If it is Your will that we should be content with the
　tame, bloodless things,
　As pale as angels smirking by, with folded wings.
　　　Oh! I know Virtue, and the peace it brings!
　　　　The temperate, well-worn smile
The one man gives you, when you are evermore his
　own:
　　And afterwards the child's, for a little while,
　　　With its unknowing and all-seeing eyes
　　So soon to change, and make you feel how quick
The clock goes round. If one had learned the trick –
　　(How does one though?) quite early on,
　　Of long green pastures under placid skies,
　　One might be walking now with patient truth.
What did we ever care for it, who have asked for
　youth,
　　When, oh! my God! this is going or has gone?

There is a portrait of my mother, at nineteen,
   With the black spaniel, standing by the garden
      seat,
   The dainty head held high against the painted
      green
And throwing out the youngest smile, shy, but half
   haughty and half sweet.
      Her picture then: but simply Youth, or simply
         Spring
            To me to-day: a radiance on the wall,
            So exquisite, so heart-breaking a thing
         Beside the mask that I remember, shrunk and
            small,
               Sapless and lined like a dead leaf,
All that was left of oh! the loveliest face, by time and
   grief!
   And in the glass, last night, I saw a ghost behind
      my chair –
   Yet why remember it, when one can still go
      moderately gay –?
         Or could – with any one of the old crew,
            But oh! these boys! the solemn way
         They take you, and the things they say –
         This 'I have only as long as you'
When you remind them you are not precisely
   twenty-two –
      Although at heart perhaps – God! if it were
         Only the face, only the hair!

If Jim had written to me as he did to-day
A year ago – and now it leaves me cold –
I know what this means, old, old, *old!*
Et avec ça – mais on a vécu, tout se paie.

That is not always true: there was my Mother – (well
at least the dead are free!)
Yoked to the man that Father was; yoked to the
woman I am, Monty too;
The little portress at the Convent School, stewing
in hell so patiently;
The poor, fair boy who shot himself at Aix. And what
of me – and what of me?
But I, I paid for what I had, and they for nothing.
No, one cannot see
How it shall be made up to them in some
serene eternity.
If there were fifty heavens God could not give us back
the child who went or never came;
Here, on our little patch of this great earth, the
sun of any darkened day,
Not one of all the starry buds hung on the
hawthorn trees of last year's May,
No shadow from the sloping fields of
yesterday;
For every hour they slant across the hedge a
different way,
The shadows are never the same.

'Find rest in Him' One knows the parsons'
    tags –
  Back to the fold, across the evening fields, like
    any flock of baa-ing sheep:
Yes, it may be, when He has shorn, led us to
  slaughter, torn the bleating soul in us to rags,
      For so He giveth His belovèd sleep.
      Oh! He will take us stripped and done,
      Driven into His heart. So we are won:
  Then safe, safe are we? in the shelter of His
    everlasting wings –
  I do not envy Him His victories. His arms are full
    of broken things.

      But I shall not be in them. Let Him take
      The finer ones, the easier to break.
And they are not gone, yet, for me, the lights, the
  colours, the perfumes,
      Though now they speak rather in sumptuous
      rooms,
      In silks and in gem-like wines;
    Here, even, in this corner where my little
    candle shines
      And overhead the lancet-window glows
      With golds and crimsons you could almost
      drink
To know how jewels taste, just as I used to think
There was the scent in every red and yellow rose
      Of all the sunsets. But this place is grey,

And much too quiet. No one here,
Why, this is awful, this is fear!
Nothing to see, no face,
Nothing to hear except your heart beating in
space
As if the world was ended. Dead at last!
Dead soul, dead body, tied together fast.
These to go on with and alone, to the slow
end:
No one to sit with, really, or to speak to, friend
to friend:
Out of the long procession, black or white or
red
Not one left now to say 'Still I am here, then see you,
dear, lay here your head.'
Only the doll's house looking on the Park
To-night, all nights, I know, when the man puts
the lights out, very dark.
With, upstairs, in the blue and gold box of a room,
just the maids' footsteps overhead,
Then utter silence and the empty world – the room –
the bed –
The corpse! No, not quite dead, while this cries
out in me,
But nearly: very soon to be
A handful of forgotten dust –
There must be someone. Christ! there must,
Tell me there *will* be some one. Who?
If there were no one else, could it be You?

How old was Mary out of whom you cast
  So many devils? Was she young or perhaps for
    years
She had sat staring, with dry eyes, at this and that
  man going past
    Till suddenly she saw You on the steps of Simon's
      house
      And stood and looked at You through tears.
        I think she must have known by those
      The thing, for what it was that had come to
        her.
      For some of us there is a passion, I suppose
      So far from earthly cares and earthly fears
      That in its stillness you can hardly stir
        Or in its nearness, lift your hand,
      So great that you have simply got to stand
      Looking at it through tears, through tears.
      Then straight from these there broke the kiss,
        I think You must have known by this
      The thing, for what it was, that had come to
        You:
        She did not love You like the rest,
      It was in her own way, but at the worst, the
        best,
        She gave you something altogether new.
        And through it all, from her, no word,
        She scarcely saw You, scarcely heard:
      Surely You knew when she so touched You
        with her hair,

Or by the wet cheek lying there,
And while her perfume clung to You from head to feet
all through the day
That You can change the things for which we
care,
But even You, unless You kill us, not the way.

This, then was peace for her, but passion too.
I wonder was it like a kiss that once I knew,
The only one that I would care to take
Into the grave with me, to which if there were
afterwards, to wake.
Almost as happy as the carven dead
In some dim chancel lying head by head
We slept with it, but face to face, the whole night
through –
One breath, one throbbing quietness, as if the thing
behind our lips was endless life,
Lost, as I woke, to hear in the strange earthly dawn,
his 'Are you there?'
And lie still, listening to the wind outside,
among the firs.

So Mary chose the dream of Him for what was left
to her of night and day,
It is the only truth: it is the dream in us that neither
life nor death nor any other thing can take away:
But if she had not touched Him in the doorway of
the dream could she have cared so much?

She was a sinner, we are what we are: the spirit
afterwards, but first, the touch.

And He has never shared with me my haunted house
beneath the trees
Of Eden and Calvary, with its ghosts that have not
any eyes for tears,
And the happier guests who would not see, or if they
did, remember these,
Though they lived there a thousand years.
Outside, too gravely looking at me, He seems
to stand,
And looking at Him, if my forgotten spirit
came
Unwillingly back, what could it claim
Of those calm eyes, that quiet speech,
Breaking like a slow tide upon the beach,
The scarred, not quite human hand? –
Unwillingly back to the burden of old
imaginings
When it has learned so long not to think, not
to be,
Again, again it would speak as it has spoken to
me of things
That I shall not see!

I cannot bear to look at this divinely bent and
gracious head:
When I was small I never quite believed that

He was dead:
And at the Convent school I used to lie
    awake in bed
Thinking about His hands. It did not matter what
    they said,
He was alive to me, so hurt, so hurt! And most of all
in Holy Week
        When there was no one else to see
        I used to think it would not hurt me too, so
            terribly,
        If He had ever seemed to notice me
        Or, if, for once, He would only speak.

EXSPECTO RESURRECTIONEM

Oh! King who hast the key
   Of that dark room,
The last which prisons us but held not Thee,
   Thou know'st its gloom.
  Dost Thou a little love this one
Shut in to-night,
  Young and so piteously alone,
   Cold – out of sight?
  Thou know'st how hard and bare
The pillow of that new-made narrow bed,
   Then leave not there
   So dear a head!

ON THE ROAD TO THE SEA

We passed each other, turned and stopped for half
   an hour, then went our way,
    I who make other women smile did not make you –
But no man can move mountains in a day.
   So this hard thing is yet to do.

But first I want your life: – before I die I want to see
   The world that lies behind the strangeness of
      your eyes,
There is nothing gay or green there for my
   gathering, it may be,
    Yet on brown fields there lies
A haunting purple bloom: is there not something in
   grey skies
       And in grey sea?
   I want what world there is behind your eyes,
I want your life and you will not give it me.

Now, if I look, I see you walking down the years,
Young, and through August fields – a face, a
   thought, a swinging dream perched on a stile –;
I would have liked (so vile we are!) to have taught
   you tears
    But most to have made you smile.

To-day is not enough or yesterday: God sees it all –
Your length on sunny lawns, the wakeful rainy

nights – ; tell me – ; (how vain to ask), but it is
   not a question – just a call – ;
Show me then, only your notched inches climbing up
   the garden wall,
            I like you best when you were small.

         Is this a stupid thing to say
         Not having spent with you one day?
No matter; I shall never touch your hair
Or hear the little tick behind your breast,
         Still it is there,
         And as a flying bird
Brushes the branches where it may not rest
         I have brushed your hand and heard
The child in you: I like that best

So small, so dark, so sweet; and were you also then
   too grave and wise?
      Always I think. Then put your far off little hand
      in mine; – Oh! let it rest;
I will not stare into the early world beyond the
   opening eyes,
         Or vex or scare what I love best.
            But I want your life before mine bleeds away –
            Here – not in heavenly hereafters – soon, –
            I want your smile this very afternoon,
            (The last of all my vices, pleasant people used to say,
               I wanted and I sometimes got – the Moon!)

You know, at dusk, the last bird's cry,
And round the house the flap of the bat's low
   flight,
   Trees that go black against the sky
And then – how soon the night!
No shadow of you on any bright road again,
And at the darkening end of this – what voice?
   whose kiss? As if you'd say!
It is not I who have walked with you, it will not be
   I who take away
   Peace, peace, my little handful of the gleaner's
      grain
   From your reaped fields at the shut of day.

      Peace! Would you not rather die
Reeling, – with all the cannons at your ear?
      So, at least, would I,
And I may not be here
To-night, to-morrow morning or next year.
Still I will let you keep your life a little while,
      See dear?
   I have made you smile.

THE SUNLIT HOUSE

White through the gate it gleamed and slept
   In shuttered sunshine: the parched garden flowers
Their fallen petals from the beds unswept,
    Like children unloved and ill-kept
      Dreamed through the hours.
Two blue hydrangeas by the blistered door, burned
   brown,
    Watched there and no one in the town
    Cared to go past it night or day,
    Though why this was they wouldn't say.
But, I the stranger, knew that I must stay,
    Pace up the weed-grown paths and down,
    Till one afternoon – there is just a doubt –
    But I fancy I heard a tiny shout –
    From an upper window a bird flew out –
      And I went my way.

THE SHADE-CATCHERS

I think they were about as high
    As haycocks are. They went running by
Catching bits of shade in the sunny street:
    'I've got one,' cried sister to brother.
    'I've got one,' 'Now I've got another.'
But scudding away on their little bare feet,
They left the shade in the sunny street.

LE SACRÉ-COEUR
(Montmartre)

It is dark up here on the heights,
   Between the dome and the stars it is quiet too,
While down there under the crowded lights
   Flares the importunate face of you,
Dear Paris of the hot white hands, the scarlet lips, the
    scented hair,
     Une jolie fille à vendre, très cher;
     A thing of gaiety, a thing of sorrow,
     Bought to-night, possessed, and tossed
     Back to the mart again to-morrow,
      Worth and over, what you cost;
While half your charm is that you are
Withal, like some unpurchasable star,
   So old, so young and infinite and lost.

It is dark on the dome-capped hill,
   Serenely dark, divinely still,
Yet here is the Man who bought you first
   Dying of his immortal smart,
Your Lover, the King with the broken heart,
   Who while you, feasting, drink your fill,
     Pass round the cup
     Not looking up,
Calls down to you, 'I thirst.'

'A king with a broken heart! *Mon Dieu!*
    One breaks so many, *cela peut se croire,*
To remember all *c'est la mer à boire,*
    And the first, *mais comme c'est vieux.*
Perhaps there is still some keepsake – or
    One has possibly sold it for a song:
On ne peut pas toujours pleurer les morts,
    And this One – He has been dead so long!'

SONG

Love, Love to-day, my dear,
  Love is not always here;
Wise maids know how soon grows sere
  The greenest leaf of Spring;
    But no man knoweth
    Whither it goeth
    When the wind bloweth
     So frail a thing.

Love, Love, my dear, to-day,
  If the ship's in the bay,
If the bird has come your way
  That sings on summer trees;
    When his song faileth
    And the ship saileth
    No voice availeth
     To call back these.

SATURDAY MARKET

Bury your heart in some deep green hollow
   Or hide it up in a kind old tree
Better still, give it the swallow
   When she goes over the sea.

In Saturday Market there's eggs a 'plenty
   And dead-alive ducks with their legs tied down,
Grey old gaffers and boys of twenty –
   Girls and the women of the town –
Pitchers and sugar-sticks, ribbons and laces,
   Posies and whips and dicky-birds' seed,
Silver pieces and smiling faces,
   In Saturday Market they've all they need.

What were you showing in Saturday Market
   That set it grinning from end to end
Girls and gaffers and boys of twenty – ?
   Cover it close with your shawl, my friend –
Hasten you home with the laugh behind you,
   Over the down –, out of sight,
Fasten your door, though no one will find you
   No one will look on a Market night.

See, you, the shawl is wet, take out from under
   The red dead thing –. In the white of the moon
On the flags does it stir again? Well, and no wonder!
   Best make an end of it; bury it soon.

If there is blood on the hearth who'll know it?
  Or blood on the stairs,
When a murder is over and done why show it?
  In Saturday Market nobody cares.

Then lie you straight on your bed for a short, short
    weeping
  And still, for a long, long rest,
There's never a one in the town so sure of sleeping
  As you, in the house on the down with a hole in
    your breast.

  Think no more of the swallow,
    Forget, you, the sea,
Never again remember the deep green hollow
  Or the top of the kind old tree!

ARRACOMBE WOOD

Some said, because he wud'n spaik
   Any words to women but Yes and No,
Nor put out his hand for Parson to shake
   He mun be bird-witted. But I do go
   By the lie of the barley that he did sow,
And I wish no better thing than to hold a rake
   Like Dave, in his time, or to see him mow.

Put up in churchyard a month ago,
'A bitter old soul,' they said, but it wadn't so.
His heart were in Arracombe Wood where he'd used
   to go
To sit and talk wi' his shadder till sun went low,
Though what it was all about us'll never know.
   And there baint no mem'ry in the place
   Of th' old man's footmark, nor his face;
   Arracombe Wood do think more of a crow –
'Will be violets there in the Spring: in Summer time
   the spider's lace;
   And come the Fall, the whizzle and race
Of the dry, dead leaves when the wind gies chase;
   And on the Eve of Christmas, fallin' snow.

SEA LOVE

Tide be runnin' the great world over:
    T'was only last June month I mind that we
Was thinkin' the toss and the call in the breast of the
    lover
    So everlastin' as the sea.

Heer's the same little fishes that sputter and swim,
    Wi' the moon's old glim on the grey, wet sand;
An' him no more to me nor me to him
    Than the wind goin' over my hand.

THE ROAD TO KÉRITY

Do you remember the two old people we passed on the
    road to Kérity,
Resting their sack on the stones, by the drenched
    wayside,
Looking at us with their lightless eyes through the
    driving rain, and then out again
To the rocks, and the long white line of the tide:
Frozen ghosts that were children once, husband and
    wife, father, and mother,
Looking at us with those frozen eyes; have you ever
    seen anything quite so chilled or so old?
            But we – with our arms about each other,
            We did not feel the cold!

I HAVE BEEN THROUGH THE GATES

His heart, to me, was a place of palaces and pinnacles
    and shining towers;
I saw it then as we see things in dreams, – I do not
    remember how long I slept;
I remember the trees, and the high, white walls, and
    how the sun was always on the towers;
The walls are standing to-day, and the gates: I have
    been through the gates, I have groped, I have crept
Back, back. There is dust in the streets, and blood;
    they are empty; darkness is over them;
His heart is a place with the lights gone out, forsaken
    by great winds and the heavenly rain, unclean and
    unswept,
Like the heart of the holy city, old, blind, beautiful
    Jerusalem,
        Over which Christ wept.

THE CENOTAPH

Not yet will those measureless fields be green again
Where only yesterday the wild, sweet, blood of
    wonderful youth was shed;
There is a grave whose earth must hold too long, too
    deep a stain,
Though for ever over it we may speak as proudly as
    we may tread.
But here, where the watchers by lonely hearths from the
    thrust of an inward sword have more slowly bled,
We shall build the Cenotaph: Victory, winged, with
    Peace, winged too, at the column's head.
And over the stairway, at the foot – oh! here, leave
    desolate, passionate hands to spread
Violets, roses, and laurel, with the small, sweet,
    twinkling country things
Speaking so wistfully of other Springs,
From the little gardens of little places where son or
    sweetheart was born and bred.
In splendid sleep, with a thousand brothers
        To lovers, to mothers
        Here, too, lies he:
Under the purple, the green, the red,
It is all young life: it must break some women's hearts
    to see
Such a brave, gay coverlet to such a bed!
Only, when all is done and said,
God is not mocked and neither are the dead.

For this will stand in our Market-place –
   Who'll sell, who'll buy
   (Will you or I
Lie each to each with the better grace)?
While looking into every busy whore's and huckster's
   face
As they drive their bargains, is the Face
Of God: and some young, piteous, murdered face.

IN THE FIELDS

Lord, when I look at lovely things which pass,
  Under old trees the shadows of young leaves
Dancing to please the wind along the grass,
  Or the gold stillness of the August sun on the
  August sheaves;
Can I believe there is a heavenlier world than this?
  And if there is
Will the strange heart of any everlasting thing
  Bring me these dreams that take my breath away?
They come at evening with the home-flying rooks and
  the scent of hay,
  Over the fields. They come in Spring.

FROM A WINDOW

Up here, with June, the sycamore throws
    Across the window a whispering screen;
I shall miss the sycamore more, I suppose,
Than anything else on this earth that is out in green.
    But I mean to go through the door without fear,
    Not caring much what happens here
        When I'm away: –
How green the screen is across the panes
    Or who goes laughing along the lanes
With my old lover all the summer day.

NOT FOR THAT CITY

Not for that city of the level sun,
    Its golden streets and glittering gates ablaze –
    The shadeless, sleepless city of white days,
White nights, or nights and days that are as one –
We weary, when all is said, all thought, all done.
    We strain our eyes beyond this dusk to see
    What, from the threshold of eternity
We shall step into. No, I think we shun
The splendour of that everlasting glare,
   The clamour of that never-ending song.
   And if for anything we greatly long,
It is for some remote and quiet stair
    Which winds to silence and a space of sleep
    Too sound for waking and for dreams too deep.

ROOMS

I remember rooms that have had their part
  In the steady slowing down of the heart.
The room in Paris, the room at Geneva,
The little damp room with the seaweed smell,
And that ceaseless maddening sound of the tide –
  Rooms where for good or for ill – things died.
But there is the room where we two lie dead,
Though every morning we seem to wake and might
  just as well seem to sleep again
  As we shall somewhere in the other quieter, dustier
  bed
  Out there in the sun – in the rain.

MONSIEUR QUI PASSE
(Quai Voltaire)

A purple blot against the dead white door
In my friend's rooms, bathed in their vile pink light,
I had not noticed her before
She snatched my eyes and threw them back at me:
She did not speak till we came out into the night,
Paused at this bench beside the kiosk on the quay.

God knows precisely what she said –
I left to her the twisted skein,
Though here and there I caught a thread, –
Something, at first, about 'the lamps along the Seine,
And Paris, with that witching card of Spring
Kept up her sleeve, – why you could see
The trick done on these freezing winter nights!
While half the kisses of the Quay –
Youth, hope, – the whole enchanted string
Of dreams hung on the Seine's long line of lights.'

Then suddenly she stripped, the very skin
Came off her soul, – a mere girl clings
Longer to some last rag, however thin,
When she has shown you – well – all sorts of things:
'If it were daylight – oh! one keeps one's head –
But fourteen years! – No one has ever guessed –
The whole thing starts when one gets to bed –
Death? – If the dead would tell us they had rest!

But your eyes held it as I stood there by the door –
One speaks to Christ – one tries to catch His
  garment's hem –
One hardly says as much to Him – no more:
It was not you, it was your eyes – I spoke to them.'

She stopped like a shot bird that flutters still,
And drops, and tries to run again, and swerves.
The tale should end in some walled house upon a hill.
My eyes, at least, won't play such havoc there, –
Or hers – But she had hair! – blood dipped in gold;
And here she left me throwing back the first odd
  stare.
Some sort of beauty once, but turning yellow, getting
  old.
Pouah! These women and their nerves!
God! but the night is cold!

His dust looks up to the changing sky
    Through daisies' eyes;
      And when a swallow flies
        Only so high
    He hears her going by
  As daisies do. He does not die
In this brown earth where he was glad enough to lie.

    But looking up from that other bed,
'There is something more my own,' he said,
Than hands or feet or this restless head
  That must be buried when I am dead.
The Trumpet may wake every other sleeper.
    Do dreams lie deeper – ?
      And what sunrise
When these are shut shall open their little eyes?
They are my children, they have very lovely faces –
  And how does one bury the breathless dreams?
  They are not of the earth and not of the sea,
They have no friends here but the flakes of the falling snow;
    You and I will go down two paces –
      Where do they go?'

DOMUS CAEDET ARBOREM

Ever since the great planes were murdered at the end
    of the gardens
    The city, to me, at night has the look of a Spirit
    brooding crime;
As if the dark houses watching the trees from dark
    windows
        Were simply biding their time.

FIN DE FÊTE

Sweetheart, for such a day
  One mustn't grudge the score;
Here, then, it's all to pay,
  It's Good-night at the door.

Good-night and good dreams to you, –
  Do you remember the picture-book thieves
Who left two children sleeping in a wood the long
  night through,
    And how the birds came down and covered them
    with leaves?

So you and I should have slept, – But now,
  Oh, what a lonely head!
With just the shadow of a waving bough
  In the moonlight over your bed.

AGAIN

One day, not here, you will find a hand
   Stretched out to you as you walk down some
   heavenly street;
You will see a stranger scarred from head to feet;
But when he speaks to you you will not understand,
Nor yet who wounded him nor why his wounds are
   sweet.
   And saying nothing, letting go his hand,
   You will leave him in the heavenly street –
     So we shall meet!

EPITAPH

He loved gay things
    Yet with the brave
He laughed when he was covered with grey wings,
– Asking the darkest angel for bright things
    And the angel gave –
So with a smile he overstepped the grave.

I will not count the years – there are days too –
    And to-night again I have said
  'What if you should be lying dead?'
Well, if it were so, I could only lay my head
    Quietly on the pillow of my bed
    Thinking of Him on whom poor sufferers cried
    Suffering Himself so much before He died:
    And then of Judas walking three years by His side –
    How Judas kissed Him – how He was crucified.
        Always when I see you
          I see those two;
        Oh! God it is true
We do not, all of us, know what we do;
        But Judas knew.

I SO LIKED SPRING

I so liked Spring last year
    Because you were here; –
      The thrushes too –
Because it was these you so liked to hear –
      I so liked you.

    This year's a different thing, –
      I'll not think of you.
But I'll like Spring because it is simply Spring
      As the thrushes do.

HERE LIES A PRISONER

Leave him: he's quiet enough: and what matter
    Out of his body or in, you can scatter
The frozen breath of his silenced soul, of his outraged
  soul to the winds that rave:
Quieter now than he used to be, but listening still to
  the magpie chatter
    Over his grave.

MAY, 1915

Let us remember Spring will come again
    To the scorched, blackened woods, where the
      wounded trees
Wait, with their old wise patience for the heavenly
    rain,
  Sure of the sky: sure of the sea to send its healing
  breeze,
      Sure of the sun. And even as to these
        Surely the Spring, when God shall please,
      Will come again like a divine surprise
To those who sit to-day with their great Dead, hands in
  their hands, eyes in their eyes,
At one with Love, at one with Grief: blind to the
  scattered things and changing skies.

JUNE, 1915

Who thinks of June's first rose to-day?
    Only some child, perhaps, with shining eyes and
      rough bright hair will reach it down
In a green sunny lane, to us almost as far away
  As are the fearless stars from these veiled lamps of
    town.
  What's little June to a great broken world with eyes
    gone dim
From too much looking on the face of grief, the face
    of dread?
  Or what's the broken world to June and him
Of the small eager hand, the shining eyes, the rough
    bright head?

NE ME TANGITO

'This man . . . would have known who and what manner of woman this is: for she is a sinner.' – *S. Luke* vii. 39

Odd, *You* should fear the touch,
 The first that I was ever ready to let go,
 I, that have not cared much
For any toy I could not break and throw
To the four winds when I had done with it. You need
 not fear the touch,
Blindest of all the things that I have cared for very
 much
In the whole gay, unbearable, amazing show.

True – for a moment – no, dull heart, you were too
 small,
Thinking to hide the ugly doubt behind that hurried
 puzzled little smile:
Only the shade, was it, you saw? but still the shade of
 something vile:
  Oddest of all!
So I will tell you this. Last night, in sleep,
Walking through April fields I heard the far-off bleat
 of sheep
And from the trees about the farm, not very high,
A flight of pigeons fluttered up into an early evening
 mackerel sky.
  Someone stood by and it was you:
  About us both a great wind blew.

My breast was bared
But sheltered by my hair
I found you, suddenly, lying there,
Tugging with tiny fingers at my heart, no more afraid:
The weakest thing, the most divine
That ever yet was mine,
Something that I had strangely made,
So then it seemed –
The child for which I had not looked or ever cared,
Of whom, before, I had never dreamed.

OLD SHEPHERD'S PRAYER

Up to the bed by the window, where I be lyin',
Comes bells and bleat of the flock wi' they two
    children's clack.
Over, from under the eaves there's the starlings flyin',
And down in yard, fit to burst his chain, yapping out
    at Sue I do hear young Mac.

Turning around like a falled-over sack
I can see team ploughin' in Whithy-bush field and
    meal carts startin' up road to Church-Town;
Saturday afternoon the men goin' back
And the women from market, trapin' home over the
    down.

Heavenly Master, I wud like to wake to they same
    green places
Where I be know'd for breakin' dogs and follerin'
    sheep.
And if I may not walk in th' old ways and look on th'
    old faces
I wud sooner sleep.

MY HEART IS LAME

My heart is lame with running after yours so fast
     Such a long way,
Shall we walk slowly home, looking at all the things
  we passed
     Perhaps to-day?

Home down the quiet evening roads under the quiet
  skies,
     Not saying much,
You for a moment giving me your eyes
     When you could bear my touch.

But not to-morrow. This has taken all my breath;
     Then, though you look the same,
There may be something lovelier in Love's face in
  death
As your heart sees it, running back the way we came;
     My heart is lame.

ON YOUTH STRUCK DOWN
(From an unfinished elegy)

Oh! Death what have you to say?
  'Like a bride – like a bride-groom they ride away:
You shall go back to make up the fire,
To learn patience – to learn grief,
To learn sleep when the light has quite gone out of
    your earthly skies,
But they have the light in their eyes
    To the end of their day.'

THE TREES ARE DOWN

– and he cried with a loud voice:
Hurt not the earth, neither the sea, nor the trees –
(Revelation)

They are cutting down the great plane-trees at the end
    of the gardens.
For days there has been the grate of the saw, the swish
    of the branches as they fall,
The crash of trunks, the rustle of trodden leaves,
With the 'Whoops' and the 'Whoas,' the loud common
    talk, the loud common laughs of the men, above it all.

I remember one evening of a long past Spring
Turning in at a gate, getting out of a cart, and finding
    a large dead rat in the mud of the drive.
I remember thinking: alive or dead, a rat was a god-
    forsaken thing,
But at least, in May, that even a rat should be alive.

The week's work here is as good as done. There is just
    one bough
    On the roped bole, in the fine grey rain,
      Green and high
      And lonely against the sky.
        (Down now! –)
      And but for that,
      If an old dead rat
Did once, for a moment, unmake the Spring, I might
    never have thought of him again.

It is not for a moment the Spring is unmade to-day;
These were great trees, it was in them from root to
   stem:
When the men with the 'Whoops' and the 'Whoas'
   have carted the whole of the whispering loveliness
   away
Half the Spring, for me, will have gone with them.

It is going now, and my heart has been struck with
   the hearts of the planes;
Half my life it has beat with these, in the sun, in the
   rains,
     In the March wind, the May breeze,
In the great gales that came over to them across the
   roofs from the great seas.
     There was only a quiet rain when they were
       dying;
     They must have heard the sparrows flying,
And the small creeping creatures in the earth where
   they were lying –
     But I, all day, I heard an angel crying:
      'Hurt not the trees.'

SMILE, DEATH

Smile, Death, see I smile as I come to you
    Straight from the road and the moor that I leave
      behind,
Nothing on earth to me was like this wind-blown
    space,
Nothing was like the road, but at the end there was a
    vision or a face
    And the eyes were not always kind.

Smile, Death, as you fasten the blades to my feet for
    me,
On, on let us skate past the sleeping willows dusted
    with snow;
Fast, fast down the frozen stream, with the moor and
    the road and the vision behind,
    (Show me your face, why the eyes are kind!)
And we will not speak of life or believe in it or
    remember it as we go.

THE RAMBLING SAILOR

In the old back streets o' Pimlico,
On the docks at Monte Video,
At the Ring o' Bells on Plymouth Hoe
He'm arter me now wherever I go.
An' dirty nights when the wind do blow
I can hear him sing-songin' up from sea:
Oh! no man nor woman's bin friend to me
An' to-day I'm feared wheer to-morrow I'll be,
Sin' the night the moon lay whist and white
On the road goin' down to the Lizard Light
When I heard him hummin' behind me.

'Oh! look, boy, look in your sweetheart's eyes
    So deep as sea an' so blue as skies;
An' 'tis better to kiss than to chide her.
If they tell 'ee no tales, they'll tell 'ee no lies
        Of the little brown mouse
        That creeps into the house
To lie sleepin' so quiet beside her.

'Oh! hold 'ee long, but hold 'ee light
Your true man's hand when you find him,
He'll help 'ee home on a darksome night
        Wi' a somethin' bright
        That he'm holdin' tight
In the hand that he keeps behind him.

'Oh! sit 'ee down to your whack o' pies,
So hot's the stew and the brew likewise,
But whiles you'm scrapin' the plates and dishes,
A'gapin' down in the shiversome sea
For the delicate mossels inside o' we
Theer's a passel o' hungry fishes.'

At the *Halte des Marins* at *Saint Nazaire*
I cussed him, sittin' astride his chair;
An' Christmas Eve on the Mary Clare
I pitched him a'down the hatch-way stair.
But 'Shoutin' and cloutin's nothing to me,
Nor the hop nor the skip nor the jump,' says he,
'For I be walkin' on every quay –'

'So look, boy, look in the dear maid's eyes
And take the true man's hand
And eat your fill o' your whack o' pies
Till you'm starin' up wheer the sea-crow flies
Wi' your head lyin' soft in the sand.'

THE CALL

From our low seat beside the fire
   Where we have dozed and dreamed and watched
     the glow
  Or raked the ashes, stopping so
We scarcely saw the sun or rain
  Above, or looked much higher
Than this same quiet red or burned-out fire.

     To-night we heard a call,
     A rattle on the window-pane,
     A voice on the sharp air,
And felt a breath stirring our hair,
  A flame within us: Something swift and tall
Swept in and out and that was all.

Was it a bright or a dark angel? Who can know?
  It left no mark upon the snow,
    But suddenly it snapped the chain
    Unbarred, flung wide the door
    Which will not shut again;
And so we cannot sit here any more.

     We must arise and go:
    The world is cold without
    And dark and hedged about
With mystery and enmity and doubt,
     But we must go
    Though yet we do not know
Who called, or what marks we shall leave upon the
  snow.

ABSENCE

Sometimes I know the way
  You walk, up over the bay;
It is a wind from that far sea
That blows the fragrance of your hair to me.

Or in this garden when the breeze
  Touches my trees
To stir their dreaming shadows on the grass
  I see you pass.

In sheltered beds, the heart of every rose
  Serenely sleeps to-night. As shut as those
Your guarded heart; as safe as they from the beat, beat
Of hooves that tread dropped roses in the street.

  Turn never again
  On these eyes blind with a wild rain
Your eyes; they were stars to me. –
  There are things stars may not see.

But call, call, and though Christ stands
  Still with scarred hands
Over my mouth, I must answer. So,
I will come – He shall let me go!

TO A CHILD IN DEATH

You would have scoffed if we had told you yesterday
   Love made us feel, or so it was with me, like some
     great bird
     Trying to hold and shelter you in its strong wing; –
A gay little shadowy smile would have tossed us back
  such a solemn word,
     And it was not for that you were listening
     When so quietly you slipped away
With half the music of the world unheard.
What shall we do with this strange summer, meant for you, –
     Dear, if we see the winter through
     What shall be done with spring?
This, this is the victory of the Grave; here is death's sting,
That it is not strong enough, our strongest wing.

But what of His who like a Father pitieth?
His Son was also, once, a little thing,
The wistfullest child that ever drew breath,
Chased by a sword from Bethlehem and in the busy
  house at Nazareth
Playing with little rows of nails, watching the
  carpenter's hammer swing,
Long years before His hands and feet were tied
And by a hammer and the three great nails He died,
     Of youth, of Spring,
Of sorrow, of loneliness, of victory the King,
     Under the shadow of that wing.

MOORLAND NIGHT

My face is against the grass – the moorland grass is
wet –
   My eyes are shut against the grass, against my lips
     there are the little blades,
         Over my head the curlews call,
And now there is the night wind in my hair;
My heart is against the grass and the sweet earth; – it
has gone still, at last.
         It does not want to beat any more,
          And why should it beat?
         This is the end of the journey;
          The Thing is found.

         This is the end of all the roads –
     Over the grass there is the night-dew
And the wind that drives up from the sea along the
moorland road;
     I hear a curlew start out from the heath
      And fly off, calling through the dusk,
        The wild, long, rippling call.
     The Thing is found and I am quiet with the earth.
Perhaps the earth will hold it, or the wind, or that
bird's cry,
But it is not for long in any life I know. This cannot
stay,
Not now, not yet, not in a dying world, with me, for
very long.

I leave it here:
And one day the wet grass may give it back –
One day the quiet earth may give it back –
The calling birds may give it back as they go by –
To someone walking on the moor who starves for love
and will not know
Who gave it to all these to give away;
Or, if I come and ask for it again,
Oh! then, to me.

AN ENDING

You know that road beside the sea,
    Walled by the wavin' wheat,
Which winds down to the little town,
    Wind-blown and grey and up the crooked street?
        We'd used to meet
Just at the top, and when the grass was trodden down
    'Twas by our feet.
        We'd used to stand
And watch the clouds like a great fleet
    Sail over the sea and over land,
        And the gulls dart
Above our heads: and by the gate
    At the road's end, when et was late
And all the ships was showing lights on quiet nights,
        We'd used to part.

So, Sir, you think I've missed my way,
    There's nothing but the Judgment Seat –
But ef I pray perhaps I may – what's that you say –
    A golden street?
        Give me the yellow wheat!
    Et edn't *there* we'm goin' to meet!
No, I'm not mazed, I make no doubt
    That ef we don't my soul goes out
'Most like a candle in the everlasting dark.
        And what's the odds? 'Twas just a spark

Alight for her.
   I tell you, Sir,
That God He made et brave and plain,
   Sin' He knows better than yon Book
     What's in a look
   You'd go to Hell to get again.

Another hour? An hour to wait – !
   I sim I'll meet her at the gate –
You know that road beside the sea –
   The crooked street – the wavin' wheat – ?
(What's that? A lamp! Et made me start –)
   That's where our feet – we'd used to meet – on
     quiet nights –
My God! the ships es showing lights! –
     We'd used – to part.

A FAREWELL

Remember me and smile, as smiling too,
  I have remembered things that went their way –
  The dolls with which I grew too wise to play –
Or over-wise – and kissed, as children do,
And so dismissed them; yes, even as you
  Have done with this poor piece of painted clay –
  Not wantonly, but wisely, shall we say?
As one who, haply, tunes his heart anew.

Only I wish her eyes may not be blue,
  The eyes of the new angel. Ah! she may
Miss something that I found, – perhaps the clue
To those long silences of yours, which grew
  Into one word. And should she not be gay,
  Poor lady! Well, she too must have her day!

A QUESTION

If Christ was crucified – Ah! God, are we
   Not scoured, tormented, mocked and called to pay
   The sin of ages in our little day –
Has man no crown of thorns, no Calvary,
Though Christ has tasted of his agony?
   We knew no Eden and the poisoned fruit
   We did not pluck, yet from the bitter root
We sprang, maimed branches of iniquity.

Have we who share the heritage accurst
   Wrought nothing? Tainted to the end of time,
The last frail souls still suffer for the first
   Blind victims of an everlasting crime.
Ask of the Crucified, Who hangs enthroned,
If man – oh! God, man too has not atoned!

'THERE SHALL BE NO NIGHT THERE'
In the Fields

Across these wind-blown meadows I can see
   The far off glimmer of the little town,
   And feel the darkness slowly shutting down
To lock from day's long glare my soul and me.
   Then through my blood the coming mystery
Of night steals to my heart and turns my feet
Toward that chamber in the lamp-lit street,
   Where waits the pillow of thy breast and thee.

'There shall be no night there' – no curtained pane
   To shroud love's speechlessness and loose thy hair
For kisses swift and sweet as falling rain.
   No soft release of life – no evening prayer.
   Nor shall we waking greet the dawn, aware
That with the darkness we may sleep again.

LEFT BEHIND

Wilt thou have pity? intercede for me.
　So near, at last thou standest to the throne,
　Thou mayest call for mercy on thine own,
As here thine own for mercy calls on thee.
Fling then my soul, thy soul, upon its knee;
　Bestir these lips of mine for me to pray;
　Release this spirit from its tortured clay,
Remembering that thine, its mate, is free.

I wait thy summons on a swaying floor,
　Within a room half darkness and half glare.
　I cannot stir – I cannot find the stair –
　　Thrust hands upon my heart – ; it clogs my
feet,
　　As drop by drop it drains. I stand and beat –
I stand and beat my heart against the door.